Doozandohnt

Illustrated guide to
Training Parents

Published by Top That! Publishing plc
Copyright © 2010 Top That! Publishing plc
Tide Mill Way, Woodbridge, Suffolk, IP12 1AP, UK
www.topthatpublishing.com
Top That! is a registered trademark of Top That! Publishing plc

This edition published in Great Britain in 2010 by Top That! Publishing plc,
Marine House, Tide Mill Way,
Woodbridge, Suffolk, IP12 1AP, UK
www.topthatpublishing.com
0 2 4 6 8 9 7 5 3 1

Creative Director – Simon Couchman
Editorial Director – Daniel Graham
Art Editor – Matt Denny

Written and illustrated by Andrew Pinder

ISBN 978-1-84956-081-8

A catalogue record for this book is available from the British Library
Printed and bound in China

Foreword

You can choose your friends, but, unfortunately, you can't choose your family. Badly behaved parents are a growing problem in our society with many offspring experiencing embarrassing episodes, tantamount to cruelty, at the hands of their misguided guardians. Following years of painstaking research, at the Top That! Institute of Behavioural Studies, I have devised a patented, parent training programme that will help to modify inappropriate behaviour. Now, YOU can reap the benefits of my studies by reading this learnamologically enhanced book.

During my research, I learnt that the most important thing for parents to learn is their place in the family hierarchy. Just like a dog, your parents must learn your rules and how to behave in an agreeable, social manner towards you and your friends. In order to better explain how to discourage bad parental behaviour, I have teamed up with the world's best doodle artist, Andrew Pinder, and have presented my findings as simple 'Do' and 'Don't' instructions, with a life-enriching dollop of humour. This book will help you to train your parents on all aspects of your life – clothes, music, fashion, friends, holidays, allowance – and, according to statistics, will improve parents, on average, by 56%.

I hope that you enjoy reading my findings, and that they help you to make decisions, which lead to a happier lifestyle.

A cautionary note:

Reading and acting upon the advice contained in this book may have side effects. During trials, a high percentage of my test subjects reported that parents began involuntarily salivating every time the doorbell or phone rang. I deem the overall benefits of my training programme to far outweigh this minor side effect.

Dr Heinz Doozandohntz

DO help your parents by tuning in the television.

DON'T teach them how to do it themselves - knowledge pays!

DO have a quiet word with your parents about their embarrassing dancing.

DON'T be tempted to teach them a more modern style. It can have disastrous effects!

DO ask your parents to stop any embarrassing shows of affection - kissing, holding hands, pet names, etc.

DON'T extend the rule to when they are in private - it may be disgusting, but even old people like to snuggle up!

Top Tip!

Suggest that your parents buy you an MP3 player to give them some privacy!

DO be patient when your parents moan about the way you dress.

DON'T forget to look through some old albums to find pictures of when they were young. Then, leave them out!

DO try not to blush and moan when your mum shows your friends embarrassing baby photos – it will only encourage her.

DON'T slip that photo that dad took of her changing on the beach into her next work presentation – that would be going too far!

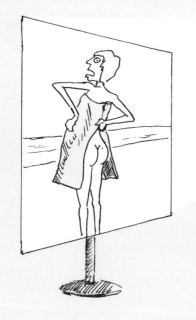

DO listen to your dad when he tells you about firework safety.

DON'T cheer if it goes wrong.

* Note: Dads mess up a lot. Try to ignore this fact to maximise earning potential

DO bond with your parents on the beach. You're never too old to play with your dad.

DON'T forget where you buried him.

DO be tolerant if your parents sometimes get a bit silly and confused.

DON'T forget to remind them about what happened the morning after. They might have forgotten.

DO listen to your dad when he tells you that you must respect teachers and other people in authority.

DON'T neglect to remind him when it slips his mind!

DO explain to your dad that his disgusting, scratchy beard makes him look like an old tramp.

DON'T use your mum's hair removal cream to get the job done! An irate dad and a mum with hairy legs is a distinct possibility.

zzzzzzzzzzzzzzz ...

DO educate your parents into being discreet when your friends are in the house.

DON'T, on any account, allow your dad to be jovial. Dads think that they are funny, but it has been scientifically proven that they are not!

TRAINING FOR FAMILY REUNIONS:

DO confirm that you will NOT...

I'm a little teapot ...

... do the party piece that you used to do when you were three

... dance

You're pretty

... sit next to your creepy cousin

I want a poo ... now

... be in charge of your youngest cousin

Is it something to do with the war?

... play charades.

DON'T ...

... let your mother take offence at everything her sister-in-law says

... let your dad get into arguments about the party games

... allow yourself to be responsible for your gran after she's had a few drinks.

Even better, **DON'T** go.

DO be nice to your parents' friends when they throw a party.

DON'T worry about telling little white lies to get you out of tricky situations.

DO nag your father about getting into shape. He'll live longer and will be able to give you financial support for years to come - result!

DON'T let him get obsessed with his appearance. A vain father can be more embarrassing than a flabby one.

DO go and sit with your grandparents, and listen to them talking about the past (you'll become a favourite grandchild and reap the rewards!).

DON'T just listen. Take notes when they tell you stories of your dad's boyhood. This information could get you off the hook when you get into scrapes of your own.

DO remember that, when your mum and dad meet your best friend's impossibly glamorous parents, they will be as embarrassed as you.

DON'T try and make your parents trendier at the last moment.

DO show your father your latest video game.

DON'T show him how to play it.

Cunning tips if you are an ONLY CHILD:

DO explain that the only way you will not feel lonely is for your parents to buy you the latest mobile phone and computer to keep in touch with your friends.

DON'T scream when your parents find another way to stop you from being lonely and tell you that you are going to have a new brother or sister.

Eeeeeek!

Cunning tips if you are an OLDEST CHILD:

DO explain that you are nearly an adult and therefore need more money, be allowed to go out more, stay up later, etc.

DON'T make a fuss when your mum takes your old toys to the charity shop.

Noooooooooo!

Cunning tips if you are a MIDDLE CHILD:

DO tell your parents that having the same amount of pocket money as your older brother or sister would slightly make up for the fact that they ignore you ...

... and it would make you feel more adult and responsible.

DON'T blame everything you do on your brothers and sisters – you'll get caught out in the end!

Cunning tips if you are a YOUNGEST CHILD:

DO say that you are not a baby and want more respect and pocket money.

DON'T expect your parents to always take your side against your older siblings.

They're always picking on me!!!!

BEDROOM TRAINING:

DO insist on your privacy. Train your parents to knock before coming into your bedroom.

DON'T go into their bedroom without knocking to show them how irritating it is. What you might see will live with you for the rest of your life.

DO point out that for your homework you need a computer with broadband connection, a television and DVD player in your bedroom. Not want, NEED.

DON'T let your parents decorate your bedroom unsupervised.

HOUSEWORK TRAINING:

DO tell them that washing-up liquid is terrible for your skin ...

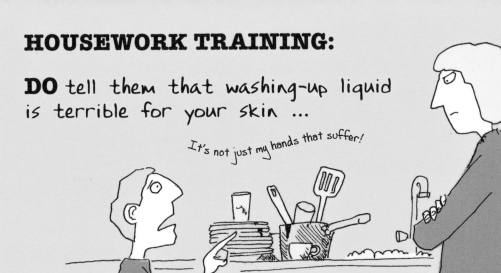

... bathroom cleaning products are bad for young people's lungs ...

... and noisy vacuum cleaners are dangerous for young ears, but ...

DON'T be surprised at your next birthday present.

TRAINING FOR A SLEEPOVER
Part I: Before The Day:

DO persuade your father to put clothes on before going to the bathroom in the morning.

DON'T let your mother show off the family photos. Hide the album.

DO make your parents remove any un-cool toys, duvet covers, etc. (You can put them back after.)

DON'T let your parents allow younger siblings to get in the way.

CELLAR

TRAINING FOR A SLEEPOVER
Part II: The Day:

DO be firm that they are NOT allowed to join in.

DON'T let your parents have noisy arguments after you have gone to bed.

DO make a list for your mum about breakfast:

Do want

 Pancakes

Proper cereal

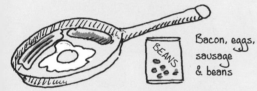 Bacon, eggs, sausage & beans

 Normal bread, chocolate spread

 Juice from a shop

 Plain plates and glasses

Don't want

Porridge

Healthy cereals

Tofu, vegetables

Bread with bits in, ANYTHING home-made

Juice from real fruit

Funny mugs

DO walk fast when you go shopping with your parents, so that they have to hurry to keep up.

DON'T slow down and give them a chance to talk to boring people.

DO ask your dad about the toys that he used to play with when you are out shopping. With a bit of luck you could steer him straight to a toy shop.

DON'T try it if your grandad is also with you, or you'll end up at the toy museum.

DO pretend that you can't hear your parents when they call out - this will stop them from looking in boring shops.

DON'T stop listening to them completely - you might miss the snack stop.

DO go shopping for school clothes with your dad – he won't have a clue what is needed.

DON'T go for a haircut with your dad – he'll get them to give you the same style that he had when he was a boy.

DO keep quiet when your parents ask what you think of their holiday clothes.

DON'T feel that you have to associate with them on the beach.

DO go through a hairstyle magazine with your mum and help her choose a less frumpy style.

Top Tip!

Parent + child bonding = praise, treats and rewards.

DON'T, whatever you do, persuade her to go for anything too extreme.

Well, what do you think?

Gulp!

DO explain the importance of having enough money on your mobile, in case of an emergency.

DON'T buy any ringtones until they have left the room.

DO offer to help with the shopping if you hate your healthy lunch.

DON'T remember the shopping list.

NEGOTIATING POCKET MONEY:

DO ... nag

... say how everyone gets more than you

... show how much prices have gone up

... explain how humiliating it is to be the class pauper.

DON'T flaunt your newfound wealth in front of your parents if you do get a rise.

Taxi! The video game arcade and quick about it!

DO explain that not to go to the rock concert would be social suicide.

DON'T tell them where to get tickets.

DO encourage your dad to come and watch you play for your team.

DON'T let him get carried away.

DO encourage your parents to book up an exotic holiday, but do your research carefully.

DON'T let them choose anywhere with a nudist beach - think of the awful holiday photos!

I feel so free!

DO tell your parents that old people flirting is sad.

DON'T flirt with everyone yourself, or you'll get a bad reputation.

DO insist that, when your parents go out to celebrate, they take you along to the posh restaurant. Not to do it would be to neglect your social and cultural education.

I've always wanted to try French cuisine

DON'T moan about the food all night.

What do you call this muck?

DO make breakfast for your parents, especially if you want to ask a favour.

DON'T let them get out of doing the washing-up afterwards - you've done your bit.

DO persuade your parents to buy you a pet – you need one for company and to teach you a sense of responsibility.

DON'T let them choose one on their own.

The man in the pet shop said that they were quite rare

HAPPY BIRTHDAY FROM MUM AND DAD

Yeah, I'm not surprised

DO wash the smelly, old family dog, if your parents ask you to.

DON'T forget to go a bit mad - this will ensure that they won't ask you to do it again.

DO smile politely when your dad tries to educate your musical taste by playing his horrible, crackly, old, vinyl records.

DON'T play them your favourite gangsta rap – they'll either hate it ...

... or worse, love it.

DO what your father says when he tells you to get off your lazy backside and mow the lawn.

DON'T fight too hard to control the mower – with a bit of luck you won't be asked again.

DO let slip, as a joke, that your father has been to prison.

DON'T worry about telling him. It will make school parent meetings a little more interesting!

The teachers were so scared, they forgot to talk about me!

DON'T argue when your dad is intent on going on an outing – it'll do no good.

I've promised your uncle that we will take cousin Billy to the zoo today

DO make sure that you are never asked to do that sort of thing again.

Where's Billy? I thought that he was with you

Who? No idea

DO remember that it's not your parents' fault if they are much younger or older than your friends' mums and dads. You can't do anything about it, but remember...

DON'T ever let the young ones and the old ones meet.

DO say if you think that you are being treated too young.

SANTA'S GROTTO

DON'T go on too much about it - there could be disadvantages.

THE DULL DICTIONARY

DICTIONARY

TRAINING FOR CHRISTMAS:

DO make your parents' Christmas presents. They will think that you have gone to a lot of trouble ... and it's cheap.

DON'T make it obvious that you have done it because it is cheap.

It's a pencil holder. Now, where's my present?

DO give your parents hints about what you would like for Christmas.

DON'T show your disappointment if you do not get what you asked for.

DO allow your dad to watch his team play ...

... but, if your favourite soap is due on make sure you see it ...

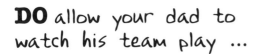

... then lose the remote control.

DO point out the educational possibilities of a visit to the new theme park.

DON'T rub it in by making your father go on the rollercoaster.

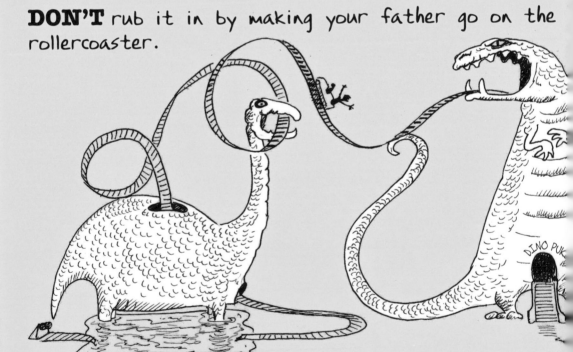